NOTE TO PARENTS

Welcome to Kingfisher Readers! This program is designed to help young readers build skills, confidence, and a love of reading as they explore their favorite topics.

These tips can help you get more from the experience of reading books together. But remember, the most important thing is to make reading fun!

Tips to Warm Up Before Reading

- Ask your child to share what they already know about the topic.
- Preview the pages, pictures, sub-heads, and captions, so your reader will have an idea what is coming.
- Share your questions. What are you both wondering about?

While Reading

- Stop and think at the end of each section. What was that about?
- Let the words make pictures in your minds. Share what you see.
- When you see a new word, talk it over. What does it mean?
- Do you have more questions? Wonder out loud!

After Reading

- Share the parts that were most interesting or surprising.
- Make connections to other books, similar topics, or experiences.
- Discuss what you'd like to know more about. Then find out!

With five distinct levels and a wealth of appealing topics, the Kingfisher Readers series provides children with an exciting way to learn to read about the world around them. Enjoy!

Ellie Costa, M.S. Ed.
Literacy Specialist, Bank Street School for Children, New York

KINGFISHER
READERS

level
5

Record Breakers

The Most
Dangerous

Philip Steele

KINGFISHER
NEW YORK

KINGFISHER
LONDON & NEW YORK

Library of Congress Cataloging-in-Publication data has been applied for.

Series editor: Polly Goodman
Literacy consultant: Hilary Horton

ISBN: 978-0-7534-7094-7 (HB)
ISBN: 978-0-7534-7095-4 (PB)

Kingfisher books are available for special promotions and premiums. For details contact:
Special Markets Department, Macmillan, 175 Fifth Ave., New York, NY 10010.

For more information, please visit www.kingfisherbooks.com

Printed in China
9 8 7 6 5 4 3 2 1
1TR/0713/WKT/UG/105MA

Picture credits
The Publisher would like to thank the following for permission to reproduce their material.
Top = t; Bottom = b; Center = c; Left = l; Right = r. Cover Shutterstock (SS)/djgis; cover t SS/Melinda
Fawyer; c SS/Steshkin Yevgeniy; b Corbis/Mike Kireev/Demotix; 2l Getty/Hermann Erber/LOOK; 2cl SS/
Steshkin Yevgeniy; 2c SS/Cheryl Ann Quigley; 2cr Photoshot/NHPA; 2r Getty/digital vision; 3l Corbis/
Denis Scott; 3cl Corbis/Alberto Garcia; 3c FLPA/Frans Lanting; 3cr Photoshot/UPPA; 3r SS/bruno
ismael da silva alves; 4 Getty/Stone; 5r Getty/Robert Mackinlay/Peter Arnold; 5bl Getty/ Photographer's
Choice; 6 Getty/Imagesource; 7 Corbis/Bohemian Nomad Picturemakers; 8 Corbis/Naturfoto Honal; 9
Photoshot/NHPA; 10 Corbis/Denis Scott; 11cl Getty/OSF; 11br FLPA/Norbert Wu; 12 Getty/Jerry Young/
DK; 13ctl KF Archive (KF); 13ctr SS/Steve Collender; 13cbl Nature/Tony Phelps; 13cbr KF; 13br Corbis/
Imagemore co.; 14bl SS/Ratikova; 15t SS/Ilya Andriyanov; 15b Corbis/Pierre Holtz/Reuters; 16 Corbis/Joe
McDonald; 17ctl SS/Gilmanshin ; 17ctr KF; 17cbl Nature/Robert Valentic; 17cbr Nature/Robert Valentic;
17b Alamy/A&J Visage; 18 FLPA/Frans Lanting; 19t KF; 19b SS/Dr. J. Beller; 20 SS/Karl W.; 21tr SS/Cheryl
Ann Quigley; 21br Getty/James Balog/Stone; 22 SS/Natursports; 23tr Corbis/Hugh Sitton; 23br Corbis/
Denis Kunkel; 24cl Getty/Vetta; 24b KF; 25 Getty/AFP; 26cl SS/Mark Yarchoan; 26b Photoshot/Moodboard;
27 Corbis/Alberto Garcia; 28tl SS/Steshkin Yevgeniy; 28b Corbis/Richard H. Cohen; 29 Getty/The Image
Bank; 30 Photoshot/Firoz Ahmed/Drik/Majority World; 31t Photoshot/UPPA; 31b KF; 32 Getty/LOOK; 33
Getty/All Canada Photos; 34 SS/bruno ismael da silva alves; 35 Corbis/Andry Prasetyo/Reuters; 36 SS/
Germanskydiver; 37tr Getty/Hermann Erber/LOOK; 37br Corbis/Mike Kireev/Demotix; 38 Rex Features/
Anthony Upton; 39t Corbis/Transtock; 39b Corbis/CSPA/NewSport; 40 Corbis/Derek M. Allan/Travel Ink;
41 Corbis/Marcelo Hernanadez/dpa; 42ll Getty/Stone; 42b Alamy/Patrick Forget/Sagaphoto; 43tr Alamy/
David Osborn; 44tl Getty/digital vision; 44b SS/EpicStockMedia; 45tr Getty/Stone; 45cr Getty/Photolibrary;
46l Getty/Hermann Erber/LOOK; 46cl SS/Steshkin Yevgeniy; 46c SS/Cheryl Ann Quigley; 46cr Photoshot/
NHPA; 46r Getty/digital vision; 47l Corbis/Denis Scott; 47cl Corbis/Alberto Garcia; 47c FLPA/Frans
Lanting; 47cr Photoshot/UPPA; 47r SS/bruno ismael da silva alves.

Contents

Dealing with danger

We learn to deal with all kinds of dangers during our lifetime. As young children, we learn to stay away from hot ovens and fierce dogs. We are taught how to play soccer and ride a bicycle without being injured. We soon find out how to keep ourselves safe.

At some time in our lives, we learn how to protect ourselves from illnesses, accidents, or sports injuries. More unusual dangers might include poisoning by plants or terrifying attacks by wild animals. We may find ourselves at risk from large natural disasters such as floods or earthquakes.

A tiger bares its teeth and snarls. This powerful big cat roams the forests of Asia.

Many of us enjoy some risk. Mountain climbers and explorers welcome adventurous challenges. Others may prefer to get their thrills from exciting movies, books, or computer games.

People can be clever and brave. They learn how to protect their bodies from harm. They try to protect other people, too, and save lives. They meet dangerous challenges and learn from their experiences.

Climbing is dangerous but exciting.

Warning signs tell us if there is danger ahead.

5

The body's defenses

Our bodies have many natural ways of protecting themselves from harm. If we hurt ourselves, our **nerves** pick up the danger signals at once. They send a message to the brain. We feel the pain and take action to stop it.

Eyelashes and eyelids shield our eyes from dust and grit. Nails protect our fingertips and toes. Skin and the **vessels** that carry blood around our body help control our temperature. This makes it less likely that we will die from extreme cold or heat.

Adrenaline helps this rider handle a dangerous situation.

When we are faced with danger, we need super powers! A **gland** in our body produces adrenaline. This substance pumps extra oxygen into our blood and makes our heart speed up. It stiffens the muscles. It helps us concentrate so that we can fight—or run away fast!

Our protection against illnesses and wounds is called the immune system. Its weapons include white blood cells, which destroy **germs**. Our body can repair itself and recover from scrapes, sprains, and even broken bones.

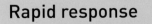

Rapid response

When we are in trouble, our nervous system can send messages to and from the brain at speeds of 330 ft. (100m) per second!

7

Don't eat these!

⚠ Beware belladonna, or deadly nightshade—it has highly poisonous berries and leaves.

We eat many different plants, but some plants are dangerous. This is because they have defenses to keep away people and animals. Sharp thorns can tear our skin, the oil on leaves causes itching, and stinging hairs can cause a painful rash. The juices of some plants, such as euphorbias (spurges), can blister the skin or damage the eyes.

The biggest risk is from plants that have berries, leaves, roots, or seeds that are poisonous to eat. They are often mistaken for harmless plants. People may become sick or even die if they eat them. Extremely dangerous plants include hemlock, foxglove, and monkshood.

Some fungi, such as mushrooms, are popular foods, but other fungi are deadly. The one that kills the most people is called the death cap. Its poison causes vomiting and extreme pain, and it attacks the liver and kidneys. It is pale green or yellowish. Young death caps are round, but the head grows and flattens to about 2–6 in. (5–15cm) across. People can mistake the death cap for other fungi that are safe to eat.

The fatal death cap fungus grows mostly in woodlands in Europe.

A dish of death

In 1534, one of the most powerful men in the world, Pope Clement VII, died after eating a death cap. Was it an accident? Many people believe he was killed by a poisoner.

DO NOT EAT!
Never eat any wild plants, berries, or fungi without checking with an adult first.

Ocean killers

Very few animals hunt humans, but some will attack people if they are in danger themselves. Animals are often the most fierce when they are protecting their young.

One of the most feared animals is the great white shark. It hunts in the warm waters of the Atlantic, Pacific, and Indian oceans. This fish can grow up to 20 ft. (6m) long. It has a sharp sense of smell, and its snout is packed with about 300 sharp teeth.

Blood in the sea

About 100 shark attacks on humans happen each year, and one-third of these are made by great white sharks.

Sharks sometimes attack swimmers, when they confuse them with their food. These attacks are rare. Each year, more people are killed by toasters than by sharks!

Many jellyfish deliver a painful sting from their tentacles. The most dangerous ones live in the Indian and Pacific oceans. They are known as box jellyfish, marine stingers, or sea wasps. They produce powerful **venom**, which they use to kill their **prey**. A really bad sting can kill a human if it is not treated. It may take just a few minutes for the venom to stop the heart from working.

The stinging tentacles of the sea wasp can trail for 10 ft. (3m).

Beach safety can save lives. Signs such as this one warn swimmers about jellyfish.

Spiders and scorpions

They are only small, but spiders and scorpions scurry and hide in dark corners in a way that often gives us a scare.

Spiders have mouthparts that end in fangs. These inject venom to help kill prey or to protect the spider if it is attacked. The most powerful spider venom can make you feel dizzy, sick, and stiff, with blurred vision. It can cause painful blisters and even kill a person.

The most venomous spiders are found in Central and South American rainforests. They are called wandering or armed spiders. Their scientific name is *Phoneutria*, which means murderer! *Phoneutria* venom affects the nerves and muscles and makes it difficult to breathe.

Phoneutria spiders like to hide in bunches of bananas. They have long legs and extremely venomous fangs.

Don't let them bite!
There are about 38,000 **species** of spiders, but only 200 or so can hurt people. In North America, watch out for black widow and brown recluse spiders. In Australia, stay away from funnel-web spiders, which can give a dangerous bite. In Africa, beware of six-eyed sand spiders.

Black widow

Brown recluse spider

Six-eyed sand spider

Funnel-web spider

Scorpions have two big pincers and a raised, curved tail with a stinger on the end that delivers a powerful venom. The most dangerous scorpion lives in North Africa and the Middle East. It is called the death stalker. Its sting can be very painful.

The curved tail of the death stalker ends in a sharp needle that injects venom.

Insect danger

There are about one million insect species. Yellow jackets, hornets, and bees can all give a painful sting. If you upset a yellow jackets' nest or a beehive, the insects may attack you in self-defense. Bees use 22 muscles to deliver just one jab. Their stinger is made up of three **barbed** daggers, which deliver venom.

Getting stung in the mouth or throat is very dangerous, so be careful if a yellow jacket is going after your sandwich! Stings are especially dangerous to people who are **allergic** to the venom.

Sting protection
Beekeepers wear special clothing to protect the body. People keep bees because they give us honey and help plants make fruit.

A yellow jacket's sharp stinger is at the end of its tail.

The desert locust, which lives in Africa and Asia, forms great **swarms** that darken the sky. Locusts never bite or sting, but they are dangerous because they eat every plant in sight, including crops. Locusts strip the land bare, leaving people and animals with nothing to eat and at risk of **starvation**.

A single locust swarm can cover a vast area, with 100 to 200 million insects per sq. mi. (40 to 80 million per km^2).

Deadly snakes

Some snakes are deadly because their bite is venomous. Others are dangerous because they coil their bodies around their prey. These are called constrictors.

About one-fourth of the world's snakes produce venom. In the warm lands where many of these snakes live, thousands of people die of bites each year.

Scientists have learned how to deal with snakebites. They take the venom from captured snakes and inject a tiny amount of it into another animal. The animal's immune system reacts against the venom, producing a **chemical**, or chemicals, to protect itself. Scientists collect the chemicals to make **antivenoms**, which can save a person's life. Unfortunately, many snakebites occur in remote country areas without easy access to doctors or hospitals.

A venomous snake shows its fangs.

The most snakebites
The most dangerous country for snakebites is Sri Lanka. On average, about 800 people are killed by snakebites there every year.

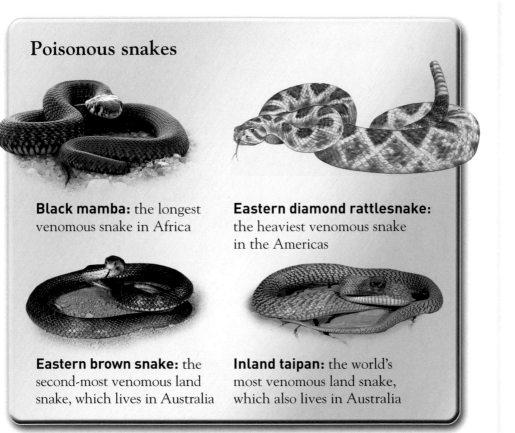

Poisonous snakes

Black mamba: the longest venomous snake in Africa

Eastern diamond rattlesnake: the heaviest venomous snake in the Americas

Eastern brown snake: the second-most venomous land snake, which lives in Australia

Inland taipan: the world's most venomous land snake, which also lives in Australia

Constrictors kill by **suffocation**. These snakes include pythons, boas, and anacondas. Reticulated pythons can kill and swallow prey up to the size of a pig. There are known cases of constrictors attacking or killing humans.

The reticulated python is the world's longest snake.

Croc attack!

One of the most dangerous animals in Africa is an armor-plated reptile, the Nile crocodile. It is 16 ft. (5m) or more long. Its weapons include a powerful tail, 64 to 68 teeth, and jaws with enormous bite power.

The crocodile can lie as still as a log for hours on end. Then, in a flash, it launches a devastating attack. It normally eats fish or birds, but it can kill large animals, too. Sometimes, it seizes people near riverbanks and pulls them under the water to drown and eat them.

The Nile crocodile has night vision and an excellent sense of smell—stay far away!

Holy crocodile!

The ancient Egyptians worshiped a crocodile god named Sobek (left). They believed that he would protect them from attack by crocodiles along the Nile River. They even made crocodiles into mummies when they died.

The saltwater crocodile lives in rivers but also travels far out to sea.

The biggest snapper of all is the saltwater crocodile of Australia, Southeast Asia, and eastern India. It can grow up to 20 ft. (6m) long and weigh up to 2,900 lb. (1,300kg).

Tooth, tusk, and claw

Many **mammals** have teeth, horns, or claws, which they use to defend themselves or to attack their prey.

A headlong charge by a wild animal can be terrifying. In Africa, the danger may come from a Cape buffalo, which has huge, curved horns, or from an angry male elephant with long tusks. The heavyweight hippopotamus, which has huge front teeth, will attack humans, overturn boats, and rampage along riverbanks at night.

The hippo's gaping jaws reveal long, sharp teeth.

Big cats such as lions, leopards, and tigers can be dangerous company even in captivity. They can attack and kill. They do not normally prey on humans, but a few do become "man eaters," especially if they are injured or short of food.

The brown bears and polar bears of the north are powerful and will swipe and slash with their claws. They are the most dangerous to us if they are disturbed when taking care of their young or when they are hungry.

Lions and bears are top hunters in their own environments.

From a safe distance

National parks and game reserves have strict safety rules. They allow people to view dangerous animals in safety. From a distance, we can respect their strength and admire their beauty.

Spreaders of disease

What are the most dangerous animals of all—
snakes, tigers, bears, or hippos? None of these. The
biggest killers are small creatures such as houseflies,
mosquitoes, and fleas, which can pass on deadly diseases.

The housefly spreads germs wherever it feeds. It lays
its eggs in human and animal waste, as well as in
garbage. It picks up all kinds of deadly diseases, which
it can pass on to humans.

Mosquitoes are bloodsuckers, and their bites are very
itchy. The bites themselves are not actually dangerous,
but the females of some **tropical** mosquito species can
pass on terrible illnesses when they bite.

The mosquito sucks
blood through long,
needlelike mouthparts,
called the proboscis.

One of the worst illnesses that mosquitoes carry is malaria. It is caused by a **parasite** that is passed on by mosquitoes when they bite. About 250 million people catch malaria every year, and about 800,000 people die from it. Doctors and scientists around the world work hard to reduce the number of deaths from malaria, and they are developing a **vaccine**.

This baby is being vaccinated against yellow fever, another dangerous disease carried by mosquitoes.

The Black Death

Rats and their fleas may pass on a terrible germ to humans. It causes an illness called the bubonic plague. More than 650 years ago, a plague called the Black Death raged through Asia and Europe. In Europe, it killed about 75 million people.

Rat flea

Quakes and waves

There is a moment of silence and then a roar and a shake. Roads crack, the ground slopes, and buildings tumble. Water and gas pipes break open. There may be floods or fires. An earthquake is taking place.

Earthquakes are caused by sections of Earth's **crust** shoving against each other. Powerful shock waves spread out under the ground. People can be buried under rubble or a **landslide**. The worst quakes may kill thousands of people.

In 2010, a terrible earthquake devastated Haiti. About 316,000 people died.

The shocks from a big earthquake under the sea can force water to rush through the ocean. This movement slows down and swells into a wall of water. The ocean is sucked out from the beaches, and a giant wave called a tsunami crashes over the coast. In 2004, one tsunami in the Indian Ocean killed more than 230,000 people.

Scientists know where earthquakes happen, but we are never quite sure when to expect one. What people can do is design buildings to survive the shaking. They can set up a warning system for tsunamis and practice what to do in an emergency.

These Japanese children wear head protection during an earthquake drill.

A big tsunami rolls inland, destroying harbors, ships, buildings, and roads.

An angry god
The ancient Greeks believed that earthquakes were caused by Poseidon, the god of earthquakes, oceans, and floods. When he stamped, the whole Earth shook!

Volcano blast

Humans face many dangers from the natural world. The most spectacular of these is the fiery **eruption** of a big volcano. Volcanoes are caused by the same violent forces deep inside Earth that cause earthquakes.

As pressure builds, stinking gases are forced through cracks in Earth's surface. Red-hot **molten** rock called lava bursts out through a volcano. The mountain can then blast apart in an eruption. This leaves a gaping **crater** and sends rocks, sparks, and ash high into the sky. Streams of red-hot lava roll down the mountainside.

Lava flows over the rocks on the Pacific island of Hawaii.

The eruption of Mount Pinatubo in the Philippines in 1991 killed more than 800 people and destroyed more than 8,000 houses.

Towns can be burned by the heat and filled with poisonous gas, or they may be buried under ash and stones. The people living there may be choked to death, burned, or buried. Clouds of ash block out the sun.

People live near volcanoes because the soil is good for farming, but they take a big risk. Eruptions are difficult to forecast. If they begin slowly, there may be time to take people away from the area and save many lives. Barriers can be built to send lava in a different direction.

The power of an eruption is massive and terrifying.

Fearsome fireworks

Sometimes a cloud of gas and rock races down a volcano at 450 mph (700km/h). It can be over 1,800°F (1,000°C) in temperature!

Storm and wind

A building can be set on fire if lightning strikes it.

Storms threaten human life. Lightning strikes cause about 24,000 deaths each year, although few are direct hits. High winds bring trees and branches crashing down.

Extreme storms with very strong winds begin in tropical ocean areas. These storms are called hurricanes, cyclones, or typhoons. They move across Earth, wheeling around a calm center called the eye. They bring lashing rain. Wind speeds can reach more than 150 mph (250km/h). They whip up high waves at sea and can cause shipwrecks.

When hurricanes reach coasts and islands, the winds may rip up trees, blow off roofs, destroy houses and crops, and overturn cars.

Tornadoes, or "twisters," are terrifying whirlwinds. They form in storm clouds, creating a funnel of dust about 330 ft. (100m) wide. The wind rips across the land, spinning at speeds of up to 300 mph (480km/h). They can be powerful enough to lift a train.

Storms can be forecast by weather scientists called meteorologists. They broadcast warnings on the radio and on television. The emergency services get ready for action. In areas where storms such as tornadoes or hurricanes are common, there are special buildings where people can take shelter.

Flood warning

Floods can happen after very heavy rains, when river banks crumble and are washed away. Homes fill with mud and swirling water. In the street, the water rises higher and higher, and only boats can be used to travel. People try to escape from upstairs windows, or they cling to the roof. Floods also happen when storms drive the ocean over low-lying coasts.

A family escapes by raft from flooding in Bangladesh.

The first danger to humans comes from drowning in fast torrents of water. Other dangers soon follow. The floods may destroy crops and damage supplies of food. Buildings may become dangerous. Flooded drains and **sewers** may spread disease.

Double danger!

Floods also affect wildlife. During floods in Australia in 2011, frogs and mice invaded many flooded homes. They were followed by venomous snakes.

Canals burst through broken levees in the city of New Orleans after Hurricane Katrina. Rescue boats traveled down flooded streets.

People build defenses against floods. They dig ditches for drainage and raise high barriers of earth and stone, such as dikes, **levees**, or sea walls. They build dams to control the flow of rivers. These bring safety, but if they break, there may be a disastrous deluge. This happened in 2005 in New Orleans, Louisiana, and more than 1,800 people died.

Large numbers of people may have to be rescued by helicopter.

Snow and ice

We all like snowball fights, sledding, and ice-skating, but extremely cold weather brings many dangers, too. Ice makes sidewalks and roads treacherous to travel on, and it's easy for accidents to happen.

Blizzards are big snowstorms with high winds. The wind piles up snow into huge drifts, burying cars. Heavy snow settles on roofs and can make them collapse. The weight of extra snow on a mountainside can cause an avalanche, a huge slide of snow that buries everything in its path.

Beep for safety!
Skiers and winter sports enthusiasts enjoy all the thrills of ice and snow, but they, too, must be well prepared. Carrying an electronic **beacon** or "beeper" helps rescue teams find them if there is an avalanche.

The human body can be dangerously chilled by wind and frost. If outer parts of the body freeze, the blood cannot flow properly. This damages the flesh, causing **frostbite**.

The human body has ways of keeping itself warm, and we can help it by wearing extra clothing, scarves, gloves, and boots in cold weather. It's safest to avoid travel if blizzards are forecast.

Walkers may not be able to see where they are going in a blizzard and can become lost.

The big heat

Long periods of hot and dry weather can turn the land into a terrifying danger zone. It takes only one spark to set bushes and trees ablaze. Fire can spread at high speed, fanned by the wind. It can surround villages, threatening animal and human life. It may take weeks to bring a fire under control.

Clearing trees from a forest in broad corridors may prevent fires from spreading. Special aircraft can drop huge amounts of water on the flames.

Black Saturday
On Saturday, February 7, 2009, 400 bush fires broke out in the Australian state of Victoria. The flames were spread by strong winds. More than 2,000 houses were burned down. It was reported that 173 people were killed and 414 injured. This terrible day became known as Black Saturday.

Long periods of very dry weather are called droughts.
Rivers and wells run dry. Crops wither and die. There
is no water for cattle. Many people become hungry and
thirsty. Babies may die because of lack of water and
nourishment. A **famine** can threaten millions of lives.

Humans cannot really control the weather, but they can
work to limit the effects of a drought. They can plant
trees, whose roots will trap moisture in the ground.
They can plant tough crops
that can survive on
little water.

A girl in Indonesia
collects precious
water from a pool.

Extreme sports

We all try to protect ourselves, but danger is also important to many of us. When we take risks, we learn how to make quick decisions. We think more carefully about how to take the right actions. Some people choose to put themselves in danger. They get a feeling of excitement from the adrenaline.

Skydivers jumping from a plane can delay the opening of their parachutes to enjoy rushing through the air in free fall. Cliff divers may dive into the sea from high rocks. They have to get the timing and angle just right to avoid injury or death.

Mountain climbers enjoy tackling dangerous challenges. They hang over sheer rock faces and cling to narrow ledges. Some prefer to climb without ropes or to climb up frozen waterfalls!

A climber uses ice picks to get a grip on the ice of a frozen waterfall.

Head bangers

Some common sports can be dangerous, too. Boxing, wrestling, ice hockey (right), auto racing, and football can all result in serious wounds, broken limbs, and head injuries. However, these sports do have rules that reduce risk.

Daredevils

Many would choose not to participate, but most people enjoy watching others take risks.

At the circus, we gasp as tightrope walkers tiptoe across the high wire. We cheer as men and women in sparkling costumes swing and leap from a trapeze. We're amazed as acrobats climb high on one another's shoulders. We may even see sword swallowers, fire-eaters, or showmen fired from a cannon. Although all performers like to play up the drama, the dangers are very real. These stunts should never be copied or tried by people who are untrained.

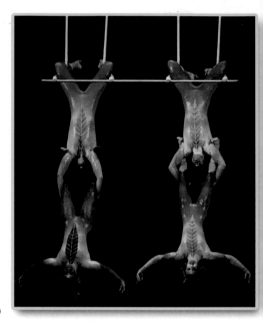

Mastering a trapeze needs years of practice and an excellent sense of balance.

The magnificent Blondin

In 1859, the French tightrope walker Charles Blondin walked on a high wire across Niagara Falls several times—with a wheelbarrow, in a sack, and with someone on his back (plus, blindfolded and on stilts on separate crossings). Once he even stopped halfway to cook an omelet!

In movies and television shows, the person who leaps from a burning car or jumps over a cliff is probably not the real actor. It is a stunt man or woman. Stunt performers learn how to take extreme risks safely. They may be helped on screen by trick camera work or by computer graphics, but their work can still be seriously dangerous.

A daredevil motorcyclist performs a trick in midair.

The stunt performer helps makes the action on the screen look really thrilling.

Dangerous work

Many people face danger every day because of their work. They may handle dangerous chemicals or hot metals, or they may operate big cutting machines. Some need special clothing for protection, such as helmets, gloves, boots, facemasks, or goggles.

Some people work in dangerous places. Steeplejacks climb high to repair church steeples, towers, and factory chimneys. Some workers stand on hanging platforms at the top of skyscrapers to clean windows or stonework. Engineers and construction workers often work high on the top of buildings and bridges.

These construction workers are building the roof of a 1,142-ft. (348-m) skyscraper in Hong Kong.

In 2010, 33 miners in Chile were rescued after being trapped underground for 69 days.

Miners risk being trapped in deep underground shafts or being killed by floods, gas explosions, or landslides. Fishing crews have one of the most dangerous jobs of all, working in storms at sea on slippery decks.

On top of the world

The world's tallest building is the Burj Khalifa in Dubai. It is 2,717 ft. (828m) high. It has built-in units that workers can use to clean the windows safely, but the top of the tower can be reached only by ropes.

Emergency!

Accidents and disasters are dangerous for the victims. They are also dangerous for the emergency services that come to rescue them. These people risk their lives to save others.

Reach for the phone!

Emergency medical services are on call 24 hours a day to deal with accidents. The main emergency services—including police, fire, and medical services—can be reached by calling a special telephone number. In the United States and Canada, that number is 911.

Firefighters battle with house fires and factory blazes and also make sure that buildings are safe from fire. They may have to deal with a dangerous chemical spill or rescue people from crashed vehicles.

Firefighters carry a hose that releases a high-pressure jet of water to put out the flames.

The job of the police is to keep the public safe. They take control at the scenes of accidents and disasters. They may face violent criminals, who sometimes carry knives or guns.

A lifeboat crew powers its way to a rescue.

Coast guards take action if there are accidents at sea. Lifeboat crews battle giant waves to search for sinking ships and to rescue the crews. They work closely with the helicopters of air-sea rescue.

Other rescue teams may specialize in rescue from mines or caves, from mountainsides, or from the rubble of a major earthquake.

Dogs to the rescue

Hundreds of years ago, dogs helped with mountain rescues in the European Alps. Dogs are still used to track down missing people in earthquake disasters and in mountain rescues.

A dog team searches a snowdrift for a missing person in the Pyrenees Mountains in France.

Living with danger

An airplane has to make an emergency landing. A racecar driver reaches a speed of more than 185 mph (300km/h). Anyone would be frightened in such dangerous situations. Fear is the most sensible reaction. It helps us imagine what may go wrong. It helps us avoid danger.

A pilot is trained to land an aircraft safely.

Surfers take time to learn their skills. They may face dangers from rip currents, huge waves, sharks, and collisions with rocks and reefs. Once they can deal with such problems, they can reduce the danger levels and make the most of the thrills.

We all have to live with dangers, whether they are big or small, exciting or scary, common or unusual. The more we learn how to deal with them, the better we understand ourselves and the world around us. We learn how to protect other people in danger, too. We learn to make the world a safer place—but perhaps not so safe that we have no fun!

Road safety is often our first lesson in dealing with danger.

We can enjoy risks if we learn to be confident but careful at an early age.

45

Glossary

allergic reacting badly to a particular chemical or food

antivenoms liquids that can be injected to treat venomous bites or stings

barbed pointed like a fish hook. A barb is a small, angled hook that is hard to pull out of something, such as skin

beacon anything used for signaling or showing the way, such as a fire, a lighthouse, or a radio transmitter

chemical another word for a substance

crater the large, bowl-shaped opening at the top of a volcano

crust the layer of rock that makes up Earth's surface

eruption the blast from a volcano. An eruption may include gases, rocks, lava (molten rock), and ash

famine an extreme shortage of food that causes widespread starvation

frostbite damage to the flesh caused by the freezing of the body

germs tiny living organisms that can make a person ill

gland one of the small organs or structures in the body that produces chemicals to make the body work properly

landslide the slip downward, such as down a mountainside, of a large amount of soil or rock

levees natural or human-made riverbanks that hold back floods

mammals animals that have hair and that feed their young on milk from their body

molten to be made liquid by heat, such as lava from a volcano

nerves fibers that carry messages between the brain and other parts of the body

nourishment food that is good for keeping the body alive

parasite an organism that lives on or in another animal

sewers large drains that carry off waste and foul water

species a group of plants or animals that breed together to produce young

starvation extreme hunger that puts life at risk

suffocation causing an animal's death by preventing it from breathing

swarms large group of insects that have gathered together to feed or breed

tropical living in the warm and wet countries near the equator

vaccine a small amount of a virus that is injected into the body to build up defenses against a particular disease

venom the poison produced by some animals that bite and sting

vessels the tubes that carry blood through the body

Index

If you have enjoyed reading
this book, look out for more in
the Kingfisher Readers series!

KINGFISHER READERS: LEVEL 4

The Arctic and Antarctica ☐
Flight ☐
Human Body ☐
Pirates ☐
Sharks ☐
Weather ☐

KINGFISHER READERS: LEVEL 5

Ancient Egyptians ☐
Hurricanes ☐
Rainforests ☐
Record Breakers—The Fastest ☐
Record Breakers—The Most Dangerous ☐
Space ☐

For a full list of Kingfisher Readers books, plus
guidance for teachers and parents and activities
and fun stuff for kids, go to the Kingfisher Readers
website: **www.kingfisherreaders.com**